Leading Sustainable Innovation

T0298922

Nick Coad
Partner at Sandwalk
nick@sand-walk.org

Paul Pritchard
Partner at Sandwalk
paul@sand-walk.org

First published in 2013 by Dō Sustainability

87 Lonsdale Road, Oxford OX2 7ET, UK

ISBN 978-1-909293-67-0 (eBook-ePub)

ISBN 978-1-909293-68-7 (eBook-PDF)

ISBN 978-1-909293-66-3 (Paperback)

A catalogue record for this title is available from the British Library.

Dō Sustainability strives for net positive social and environmental impact. See our sustainability policy at **www.dosustainability.com**.

Page design and typesetting by Alison Rayner

Cover by Becky Chilcott

For further information on Dō Sustainability, visit our website: **www.dosustainability.com**

DōShorts

Dō Sustainability is the publisher of DōShorts: short, high-value ebooks that distil sustainability best practice and business insights for busy, results-driven professionals. Each DōShort can be read in 90 minutes.

New and forthcoming DōShorts – stay up to date

We publish 3 to 5 new DōShorts each month. The best way to keep up to date? Sign up to our short, monthly newsletter. Go to **www.dosustainability.com/newsletter** to sign up to the Dō Newsletter. Some of our latest and forthcoming titles include:

- *Sustainability in the Public Sector: An Essential Briefing for Stakeholders* Sonja Powell
- *Sustainability Reporting for SMEs: Competitive Advantage Through Transparency* Elaine Cohen
- *REDD+ and Business Sustainability: A Guide to Reversing Deforestation for Forward Thinking Companies* Brian McFarland
- *How Gamification Can Help Your Business Engage in Sustainability* Paula Owen
- *Sustainable Energy Options for Business* Philip Wolfe
- *Adapting to Climate Change: 2.0 Enterprise Risk Management* Mark Trexler & Laura Kosloff
- *How to Engage Youth to Drive Corporate Responsbility: Roles and Interventions* Nicolò Wojewoda
- *The Short Guide to Sustainable Investing* Cary Krosinsky
- *Strategic Sustainability: Why it Matters to Your Business and How to Make it Happen* Alexandra McKay

- *Sustainability Decoded: How to Unlock Profit Through the Value Chain*   Laura Musikanski
- *Working Collaboratively: A Practical Guide to Achieving More*   Penny Walker
- *Understanding G4: The Concise Guide to Next Generation Sustainability Reporting*   Elaine Cohen

Subscriptions

In addition to individual sales of our ebooks, we now offer subscriptions. Access 60+ ebooks for the price of 5 with a personal subscription to our full e-library. Institutional subscriptions are also available for your staff or students. Visit **www.dosustainability.com/books/subscriptions** or email **veruschka@dosustainability.com**

Write for us, or suggest a DōShort

Please visit **www.dosustainability.com** for our full publishing programme. If you don't find what you need, write for us! Or suggest a DōShort on our website. We look forward to hearing from you.

Abstract

A MAJOR OPPORTUNITY FOR SIGNIFICANT PROGRESS on corporate sustainability is now emerging around integration with innovation practice. This book explains how this opportunity can be grasped. An overview of mainstream innovation highlights common characteristics of successful programmes including a corporate culture whose systems promote innovation. Developments such as mobile technology, social media and collaborative consumption transform the way consumers interact with companies. When viewed with emerging ideas on sustainability such as the circular economy we anticipate a major requirement for innovation. Given the common features of sustainability and innovation we see leading companies starting to integrate these agendas. We highlight the challenges faced in realising the opportunity, in particular the development requirements for sustainability executives and broader organisational learning. Sustainability should play a key role in the core innovation process of businesses. Beyond development of products with desirable characteristics it will improve innovation through wider networks, better understanding of societal expectations and, not least, providing a meaningful purpose.

....

About the Authors

NICK COAD and **PAUL PRITCHARD** are partners in Sandwalk (**www.sand-walk.org**), a business they established to support organisations with sustainable innovation.

Nick has over 20 years' experience of working in environment and sustainability. For nearly 10 years he was Group Environment Director, responsible for sustainability, at a FTSE 200 public transport company. He is particularly interested in influencing consumer behaviour and the role of new technology.

Paul was UK Head of Corporate Responsibility at RSA Insurance Group who were recognised as one of the UK's Best Green Companies 2009–2011. He is currently working as a research fellow at the University of Cambridge Programme for Sustainability Leadership focusing on new approaches to integrating sustainability into financial services.

Contents

Introduction

SUSTAINABILITY IS A RELATIVELY NEW DISCIPLINE that has developed over the last 15 to 20 years. Many commentators would argue that progress in achieving sustainable development goals has been painfully slow. While there may be a lack of political commitment to addressing issues such as climate change, there is cause for optimism in the ambitious strategies that a number of leading companies are adopting. We are entering an exciting period where some organisations have moved from a compliance mindset to actively seeking to create new opportunities by addressing environmental and social issues.

Leading organisations are now looking to change their operations, develop new products or services and develop new business models in order to meet their sustainability goals. The role of the Sustainability Executives, as we shall refer to them, is changing. There is a range of reporting lines and job titles but the emergence of Chief Sustainability Officers is a sign of growing influence at executive level. As the strategic importance of sustainability increases so the Sustainability Executives must develop new skills – particularly around personal leadership and understanding the wider organisation in order that they can inspire and lead change. This shift in importance explains why non-technical specialists will increasingly compete for sustainability roles.

The purpose of this book is to provide a practical guide to leading sustainable innovation. There is an extensive literature on both sustainability and innovation but little about innovation for sustainability.

There are some excellent books that talk about transformation to sustainability – the systemic re-engineering of capitalism.[1,2] There are even books and journals about social entrepreneurs.[3,4] However, there is very little about the role of innovation for sustainability professionals, or the role sustainability can play in supporting an overall strategy for innovation. This is the subject of our book.

We want to help those working in corporate sustainability to see the link their role has to innovation in order that they can develop more ambitious sustainability strategies in their organisation. We are also convinced that understanding sustainability will become essential to the core innovation process of organisations; as such, we hope the book will be of interest outside the sustainability function, particularly those involved in strategy, product development and human resources.

This book is a practical guide rather than an academic treatise – we avoid precise definitions and complex models in favour of broad lessons and summaries. We aren't tied to supporting a particular model or theory for either sustainability or innovation. There are no exact formulas as each organisation has a different culture and each sector its own challenges and opportunities. Inevitably there will be some bias in our selection and discussion but we have tried to achieve a fair balance, whatever that may be.

In the first chapter we aim to provide a quick overview of why sustainability requires innovation. We then look at a summary of innovation theory and thinking in Chapter 2 before pulling together the hitherto largely separate disciplines in Chapter 3. Chapter 4 discusses sustainable innovation and includes relevant case studies and Chapter 5 provides practical advice on taking these issues forward. We end by highlighting some emerging trends and outstanding challenges.

We are convinced that we are starting to see a convergence of mainstream innovation and sustainability. The commercial opportunities from sustainable innovation are enormous – the World Business Council for Sustainable Development estimates that the market opportunities created by adapting to the new global reality for sustainable living will be somewhere between $3 and $10 trillion USD per year in 2050.

We would really value feedback on the book or your thoughts on sustainable innovation more broadly – you can do this on our website **www.sand-walk.org**

We are exceptionally grateful to those people who gave up their time to be interviewed. Finally, we both would like to thank our respective families (Gillian, Finlay, Robert, Charlotte and Olivia) for their support whilst working on this project.

....

CHAPTER 1

Why Sustainability Requires Innovation

THE AIM OF THIS CHAPTER IS TO EXPLAIN why innovation is now becoming part of the role of the Sustainability Executive and is essential for those organisations that are embarking on ambitious strategies. We start with an overview of the evolution of sustainability, moving on to discuss new thinking and trends before considering what this means for the Sustainability Executive and their function.

Overview of corporate sustainability

The term 'sustainability' can be like marmite: some love it, some hate it. We have some sympathy – both of us have had to work with senior executives whose initial response is that this is fluffy, superfluous or even tree-hugging irrelevance. However, alternative terms such as 'corporate citizenship' or 'corporate social responsibility' (CSR) carry their own baggage. We use 'sustainability' here as a broad term covering management of environmental, social, ethical and governance issues. The fact that sustainability is also used in the sense of continuing profitable operation can also be useful (if at times confusing).

Sustainability emerged in the 1990s. Interface, under the inspirational leadership of Ray Anderson, helped define the term and they remain a benchmark for good practice. Their experience was instrumental in demonstrating that sustainability is consistent with business success.[5]

Sustainability management might be broadly described as comprising three levels of increasing ambition:

1. Compliance, risk management and philanthropy;

2. Efficiency improvements and enhancing corporate reputation;

3. Opportunity – generating revenue from new products, services and business models and aiming for net positive environmental impacts.

The current generation of corporate leaders – companies such as Marks & Spencer (M&S), British Telecom (BT), Unilever, General Electric (GE), Kingfisher Group, Kyocera, Procter & Gamble (P&G) and Nike – are united in their commitment to level 3 sustainability. This is not a romantic philanthropic gesture or another example of 'greenwash'. These companies have all recognised sustainability as a key strategic objective and something that is key to their future success. They realise that resource constraints, climate change and social concerns played out in a world made transparent by social media and mobile technology present profound challenges to the future success and prosperity of their own organisations as well as the societies they serve. They also recognise that they can generate new value by addressing sustainability. In ever more competitive markets with rapid changes in technology, sustainability presents a major opportunity to generate new forms of revenue.

New thinking

There are emerging ideas that are helping drive the agenda forward:

'To zero and beyond'

This sounds like a misquote from Buzz Lightyear but is a good summary of the goals that leading organisations are setting themselves – namely to have zero impact or to be restorative. John Elkington has written about these as 'Zeronauts'.[6] Some companies, such as BT, have adopted the term 'net good' to describe their aim to have a positive impact.[7] These are essentially logical developments of earlier sustainability concepts.

Two other ideas, which also have the benefit that they avoid the term 'sustainability' for those who find the term unpalatable, are of interest:

'Shared value'

Michael Porter, a Harvard professor and authority on business strategy, and Mark Kramer, wrote an influential paper that introduced the term 'shared value'.[8] This provides a great critique of CSR, and sets out the connection between social issues and competitive advantage that they claim will generate greater innovation and growth. Nestlé is one high profile corporate adopting this approach.

'The circular economy'

The circular economy is 'a generic term for an industrial economy that is, by design or intention, restorative and in which materials flows are of two types, biological nutrients, designed to re-enter the biosphere safely, and technical nutrients, which are designed to circulate at high quality without entering the biosphere'[9]. Championed by the Ellen MacArthur Foundation, it focuses on a new business model that responds to resource constraints. The Foundation has published two insightful reports setting out in detail the ideas,[9] which should be mandatory reading for the sustainability professional. The most recent report estimated that $700 billion in savings were possible if businesses apply circular economy principles to the consumer goods sector.

Neither shared value, nor the circular economy, are fundamentally different to how pioneer companies currently approach sustainability. Their biggest value may be in enabling a discussion about sustainability without the baggage of prejudice the term can invoke. The circular economy in particular is rapidly gaining traction by providing a clear focus on a solution, rather than emphasising environmental constraints. The Foundation, accompanied by a successful education programme, is rapidly gaining new supporters.

Whether a company uses sustainability, shared value or the circular economy to frame their strategies they will need to adopt radical innovation throughout all levels of the organisation – new processes, new products, new services and new business models – if they want to create new opportunities and competitive advantage from their insight. The sustainability agenda demands transformation of existing practices.

The changing skills of the sustainability function

The skills needed by Sustainability Executives, and the sustainability department, are very different for organisations moving into the third level where their aims become a strategic imperative. Levels 1 and 2 require organisations to develop new processes, standards for operations and reporting – traditional 'command-and-control' tools where technical subject matter expertise is vital. Moving up to level 3 requires Executives and teams with experience of leading innovation, managing change, creating new business plans and brands. Correspondingly, there is also a need for a greater understanding across the business in the non-sustainability functions of the environmental and social impacts of their roles.

Few corporates are currently operating anywhere near Level 3. M&S are a recognised sustainability leader, yet Mike Barry, their Head of Sustainable Business, candidly said that they are 'only 10–15% of the way to being sustainable'. In other words, there is long way to go and what lies ahead are the really challenging problems. We are entering a period that will see increased focus on innovation in sustainability. With no obvious end-point for sustainability – why stop at zero impact on the environment if you can support regeneration, and social issues and expectations will change overtime – it is unclear when this will stop or what comes next.

Convergence of sustainability and innovation?

Innovation is therefore set to play an increasingly important part in the role of the Sustainability Executive. Insights from sustainability can also support mainstream innovation processes by identifying new opportunities and filtering out bad ideas. As we discuss later, there are many similarities between managing innovation and sustainability. We are already seeing some leading companies explicitly merge responsibility for innovation and sustainability. A good example would be Nike, once a pariah of social and environmental campaigners, who have been recognised as the world's most innovative company in 2013.[10]

Nike also launched a YouTube video, 'The Making of Making', in which they state, 'Make no mistake, we hate sustainability'. Instead, the slick video says: 'We're here to unveil a new age of design, one that is about making better things and making things better.' It is a little early to announce the death of the phrase 'sustainability' – there is no reason why you can't be focused and precise in using the term sustainability – but new thinking allows you to avoid it and if like Nike, you start to align sustainability and innovation, then you can move beyond it.

CHAPTER 2

Innovation
Theory and Practice

THERE IS A VAST LITERATURE ON INNOVATION and it is definitely not our intention to provide a comprehensive review. Our aim is to provide a short overview of current thinking and practice.

When thinking about innovation it is important to separate out the generation of ideas from their subsequent implementation. There are lots of different definitions – some authors call ideas generation 'invention', while others confusingly have used 'innovation'. Successful implementation or commercial application might be termed 'innovation' or 'entrepreneurship'. We use innovation to cover both idea generation and successful implementation, but it is important to acknowledge that there is a big difference between coming up with ideas and those that go on to be successful. As one of the most famous entrepreneurs Thomas Edison said, 'vision without execution is hallucination'.

Innovation can also be described in terms of three levels:

1. Process innovation.

2. New technology, products and services – this can range from incremental improvements to existing propositions to completely new offerings.

3. New business models that result in new revenue and cost structures.

One of the biggest myths about innovation is that it is about a creative genius having a flash of inspiration in an epiphany or 'eureka' moment. The fact that innovation is typically illustrated with the light bulb doesn't help – hopefully, the association will become lose its relevance as the filament light bulb is replaced. Innovation is a discipline, which can be managed and replicated.

Innovation – it's a managed discipline

The economist Joseph Schumpeter was one of the first people to develop theories in this field. He is credited with identifying innovation as the driving force of capitalism and entrepreneurs as the agents of innovation. Schumpeter is famous for the phrase 'creative destruction', describing the process where the old way of doing things is replaced by new paradigms; he observed innovation was hard to produce and harder to maintain.

However, it was the great thinker Peter Drucker who wrote the seminal management book on the subject in 1985.[11] It is impressive given the technological advances since it was written that it retains its relevance today. The key idea in the book is that innovation is a systematic and purposeful process that can be followed by any organisation. Innovation is 'a discipline, capable of being learned, capable of being practised'. He states that innovation and entrepreneurship do not require geniuses – neither will be achieved if you wait for inspiration or the 'kiss of the muse'. Drucker acknowledges that different skills are required to support innovation as compared to traditional management techniques, but emphasises this is still a manageable process. The guidance he provides on creating a culture that rewards innovation is still as relevant today as ever.

Drucker didn't believe that innovators were necessarily inventors, capitalists or business owners. He also didn't consider innovators to be risk takers – instead he defined them by their attitude to change and said they were 'opportunity-focused'. An example of his prescience is that he believed the emergence of the entrepreneurial society would require individuals to take responsibility for their own continuous learning and development. He noted that habits and assumptions about schooling would be challenged and 'educators will have to accept that schooling is not for the young and the greatest challenge – but also the greatest opportunity – for the schools is the continuing re-learning of already highly schooled adults'. This helps explain the success of the massive open online courses (MOOCs).[12]

Disruptive innovation

Clayton Christensen introduced the term 'disruptive innovation'.[13] It describes the process, which at the time seemed counterintuitive, whereby an innovation that helps make a product or service available to new consumers at the lower end of a market can unexpectedly end up displacing the incumbent businesses. This happens because companies focus their attention on improving products and services for their most sophisticated customers where they can generate higher returns. This creates the opportunity for other organisations to innovate offerings for consumers who are less wealthy and therefore ignored by the current provider. Initially this may be lower-margin business but it provides a foothold from which a disruptive competitor can emerge with better and less expensive ways of meeting customer needs.

There are many examples of disruptive innovations, from the Ford Model T to the digital camera. They are therefore not necessarily the most 'advanced' technology rather a new combination that targets new consumers. Christensen originally used the term 'innovative technologies' but replaced this because it is the business model, rather than the technology itself, that generally creates the disruptive impact.

Organisations can respond to potentially disruptive innovations by either acquisition or establishing a competing business model. However, the speed of technology means that not all disruptive technologies start by offering an inferior product at a lower price. Navigation product makers have had to compete against maps that come preloaded for free on smart phones and are often better than the standalone device these companies sell.[14]

An interesting development is frugal innovation,[15] also referred to as 'Jugaad' after the Hindi word meaning clever improvisation. This refers to low cost innovations developed in emerging markets that are then introduced into developed economies. Such innovation inspired by scarce resources may also be why recessions have often seen the emergence of new innovative companies – to modify Plato's idiom, 'necessity is the mother of innovation'.[16]

Open innovation

Companies traditionally pursued innovation through their own Research & Development capabilities. They worked on generating a series of new ideas that would then be filtered, through a fairly linear process, to select those that would be developed into new products or services. In 2003 Henry Chesborough published an influential book that proposed a collaborative approach to innovation.[17] 'Open Innovation' involves companies working with external parties – suppliers, customers and even competitors – to increase innovation. This was a recognition that relevant specialist expertise can lie outside of the organisation. As firms operate in ever more competitive and global markets where the pace of new technology is faster, reaching outside the company boundary has become important. Consequently, innovation is now commonly seen as a collaborative process involving different organisations in an iterative and potentially complex framework.

Chesborough moved on to develop the idea of 'Open Service Innovation',[18] in which he argues businesses must think of themselves as service providers and then work with customers to co-create a more meaningful experience. This is a change from the historical focus of innovation literature on physical products and technologies. This process of open innovation both accelerates and deepens innovation (and reduces cost) by promoting the specific capabilities residing in customers and other third parties. He acknowledges that building 'experience' is harder than building a specific product since it relies on 'tacit experience', that is, learning from experience. Using both internal and external sources of knowledge and having customers participate and contribute to innovation will enable quicker testing and feedback on ideas. Chesborough maintains his own online open innovation community.[19]

The big exception to open innovation is Apple, arguably the most successful innovator of recent times. Apple is viewed as a closed and secretive organisation – they even use this to create hype around their new products. Internally though, they work across functions and clearly can connect and combine different ideas and technologies to create new products. Some have argued that they are starting to open up – they do allow apps to be built on their platform. It will be fascinating to see if this changes in the future. In general though, most businesses are seeking to work with external partners to provide expertise and skills not available internally.

This transition to open innovation demands new skills for managing collaborators whom may not work for the company. Trust between the parties is vital and must be earned through commitment to transparency. There is now a trend to sharing intellectual property to encourage new innovations.

Lean start-up

Lean start-up, a new concept defined by Eric Ries,[20] promotes quick experimentation during start-up to test whether or not customers want the product or service. Originally developed with high tech companies in mind, this approach involves developing a not yet finalised version, a 'minimal viable product' that can be tested on customers to understand what features they actually want. The concept involves continuous deployment of updates and ongoing testing with customers. Lean start-up has proven to be very successful and while not yet mainstream might well be adopted by larger companies in the future.

Managing innovation

There are a huge number of business books on the topic of innovation. A.G. Lafley, as CEO of Procter & Gamble (P&G), embraced open innovation and successfully transformed P&G into a more successful and innovative company. He co-authored a book called *Game Changers*,[21] which sets out lessons on how to create an innovation culture. This is an excellent reference that shows that large multinational corporations can be innovative provided they have supportive strategies, processes and organisational structures. Another great book that also illustrates the importance of collaboration is *The Art of Innovation*,[22] which details how the respected design and innovation consultancy IDEO encourages a creative company culture.

A good starting point for an executive wanting to understand their role in encouraging innovation is *Innovation as Usual*.[23] It highlights the following features as common to successful innovation activity:

- Open and collaborative approaches that connect not just those inside an organisation in different departments but also to external expertise.

- Providing a focus for the innovation that the organisation is seeking. Framing a problem or challenge is more effective than just asking for ideas.

- Quickly developing prototypes and experimenting to find out what customers really value. Developing ideas is an iterative process that works best when diverse groups of colleagues and external views are involved.

- Developing systems, structures and rewards that promote innovation and ensuring that this is integrated into the way the organisation works. This must recognise that innovation requires leaders to have different skills and behaviours to those in operations – for example, the ability to work collaboratively and handle uncertainty and risk. Systems must include a robust way to filter new ideas to select those with the best chance of success and the ability to fund new ideas using resources separate from the normal financial approval process.

Where Good Ideas Come From by Steven Johnson isn't a pure business book but it offers both an excellent insight into innovation and a good read.[24] Johnson eloquently considers many of the themes that appear in more academic books. Key themes include: innovation often involves recombining existing ideas and technology in new ways; collaboration is vital, as is belonging to networks with a diverse set of members, perspectives and skills; innovative ideas take time to develop and require trial-and-error.

....

CHAPTER 3

Lessons from Innovation and Sustainability Practice

THERE IS CONSIDERABLE OVERLAP IN THE CONCEPTS involved in managing innovation and sustainability, so much so that it is possible to read a book on managing innovation and swap the word 'innovation' for 'sustainability' and still find it makes sense. It's amusing to hear innovation experts refer to their subject as a 'notoriously fuzzy topic',[25] a claim frequently made of sustainability.

Innovation and sustainability activities can accordingly be broadly classified using the same categories based on the degree of change involved:

1. Incremental changes such as improving operational efficiency and changes to existing products and processes.

2. New products and services.

3. Systemic or disruptive change that may involve new business models, platforms and ultimately a transition of whole sectors/ economies.

In reality these aren't discrete categories but this structure gives a useful simplification. Innovation and sustainability also operate on a range of scales: the organisation, the value chain, sector level, regional economy, national level and global. Both subject areas are 'open-ended' in that there isn't necessarily a clear and definitive end-point – why stop at zero impact when you could lead to restoration of the environment or communities.

Common features required for managing innovation and or sustainability include:

- A clear vision and focus on the future

- Promoting new values and behaviours

- Leadership commitment

- Integration into main management process

- Managing change

- Creating networks of internal and external stakeholders

- Creating partnerships with external organisations

- Trust and transparency

- New management processes, with resources and properly aligned incentives

- Development of new knowledge and skills

- Questioning the relationships between business and society

Organisations that wish to be more innovative or implement sustainability strategies need to integrate these features into the mainstream management processes. This is not simply a case of building a new team but is something that will require change across all functions. Examples include:

- *Marketing* departments need to adopt new methods when seeking to identify the potential of new innovative products. When the post-it note was first developed at 3M marketers asked consumers if they would buy this product and received a negative response. However, when they allowed consumers to try the new product they realised that there was indeed a market. Sustainability Executives face the same challenge – environmental or social concerns may not be the top issues when consumers are asked for the reasons for their purchasing decisions but this does not mean that they are unimportant. If a follow-up question is asked about whether it is acceptable that goods are produced using sweatshops or destroy rainforests (two extreme examples) then there will be a very different response. Consumer attitudes to sustainability issues frequently contradict their actual behaviour when it comes to purchasing. This dissonance presents a real challenge and too narrow a focus on the stated preferences of individual consumers can mask underlying changes in social norms.

- *Finance* needs to develop new metrics and approaches to approving business cases for innovative ideas, which can be inherently risky. Separate funding streams are frequently made available whereby a different set of investment criteria are established. In sustainability we are starting to see the development of separate funds and emerging practice around whole-life and whole-system environmental costs.

- *Human resources* must ensure that they align incentives, rewards and development activities to support the new values and behaviours needed to achieve innovation or sustainability goals.

Organisations that embrace ambitious programmes to be more innovative or sustainable frequently report that their workforce is more engaged and satisfaction levels increase. Lynda Gratton has studied hot spots – places and times where cooperation flourishes creating great energy, innovation, productivity and excitement.[26] Her research identifies that in addition to working cooperatively and across functions or organisations (ideas that are part of established innovation theory), an 'igniting purpose' is necessary. In other words, people need to engage around a question, vision or task that they find interesting and worth engaging with. These questions are likely to be about purpose, or the 'deeper' meaning-of-life type questions, which are central to sustainability.

Sustainability clearly is an igniting purpose that is capable of engaging and motivating staff. A 2012 survey showed employees care more about sustainability than three years previously and highlighted their desire to be involved in developing sustainability strategy.[27] A 2010 study of more than 700 companies by EDF and Business in the Community found the vast majority of those surveyed said their businesses needed to do more on innovation to achieve a sustainable economy.[28] Seventy-nine percent highlighted the importance of innovation in development of sustainable technologies, products and services; 82% identified the need to work collaboratively with government, the third sector and community groups on sustainability initiatives.

Radical innovation and sustainability can be constrained by a lack of ambition and genuine commitment. Many Sustainability Executives will be frustrated by the lack of genuine commitment to sustainability. The equivalent for executives working in innovation is a lack of genuine commitment to collaboration both internally and with external partners.

We are rather fond of the title of a *Harvard Business Review* blog called 'Is collaboration the new greenwashing?', which perhaps summarises how similar the challenges are for Executives working in these separate fields.

Differences

There are nonetheless some significant areas of difference between sustainability and innovation practice that are particularly important when seeking to achieve the higher levels of sustainability:

Management processes

In Chapter 2 we showed how successful innovation is a managed process but one that requires an approach that differs from traditional command-and-control management processes. In the first two levels of sustainability, organisations typically develop and implement command-and-control processes and standards for their own direct operations and supply chains:

- Environment and energy management systems (ISO14001, ISO50001 and Carbon Standards)

- Social and ethical performance (SA8000)

- Reporting standards (GRI and AA1000)

As organisations move to the third level of sustainability the role of the Sustainability Executive changes. They will need to develop new processes and skills to inspire and lead innovation – moving away from a compliance mentality to one that is more open and collaborative.

Collaboration not engagement

Stakeholder engagement is typically the responsibility of the sustainability team. For most organisations, stakeholder engagement is about managing perception and responding to external concerns; few have explicitly used these as a tool for promoting innovation. These connections outside the organisation are an ideal starting point for creating partnerships to work on innovation challenges. Similarly, sustainable supply chain programmes, which currently work to promote best practice, are another platform that could be used for innovation purposes.

Role of public policy

Leaders in sustainability are advocates for progressive public policy to address global issues such as climate change. They argue that policy-makers need to provide long-term policy measures that encourage the transition to the low carbon economy by providing confidence for investments in new technology. Exactly how important environmental regulation has been in driving innovation to date is debatable, but most commentators consider favourable government policy essential if we are to achieve wide-scale radical changes. It's not just large corporate leaders who say this – a survey of small-to-medium-sized enterprises in the EU showed a majority thought existing regulations and structures did not provide incentives to eco-innovate.[29]

Activism

Social and environmental activism has been important in shaping the sustainability agenda and in a more connected world will continue to be a force for change. Shareholder activism, along with greater interest from the investment and pensions community (including the meaning of fiduciary responsibility), provides impetus from another direction to drive change in corporate behaviour.

Summary

Given the many similarities between innovation and sustainability it is not surprising to see that the companies leading on innovation tend to lead on sustainability as well. We are beginning to see those sustainability leaders, companies moving into the third level of sustainability, explicitly linking innovation and sustainability agendas.

CHAPTER 4

Sustainable Innovation

IN THIS CHAPTER WE ARE GOING TO DISCUSS examples from leading organisations where innovation has been undertaken specifically to achieve sustainable outcomes. The case studies aim to illustrate some of the themes and trends discussed earlier. For simplicity we consider our examples in three broad categories:

1. Process

2. New products and services

3. New business models

1. Process

Using open innovation platforms to address sustainability challenges

Open innovation platforms are now commonly used by business. Unilever are using their platform to ask for new ideas, designs and technologies for specific sustainability challenges that range from new food colours to safe drinking water and changing consumer behaviour. They also run a 'sustainable living lab' with multiple stakeholders to help them understand, in detail, a particular issue, most recently on how to mainstream sustainable living. P&G, a competitor of Unilever, is another proponent of open innovation and we later present a case study that illustrates how they have used this to develop a new sustainable product.

In 2012 Sainsbury's, the British supermarket chain, used crowdsourcing to review their sustainability strategy. This novel approach used the Green Mondays network of sustainability professionals, which includes some of their competitors, to find out what they should be doing.

Sustainability can help create new networks and partnership for innovation

Pete Markey is Chief Marketing Officer for RSA Insurance Group and is widely viewed as an influential thinker on brand, social media and innovation, not least by the Marketing Society who identified him as the UK's top marketer in their 2009 Awards for Excellence. He sees the world as one in which companies need to develop cultures that allow them to innovate quicker and smarter. 'This is where sustainability comes in', explains Pete, 'it's part of the role of the corporate sustainability function to act as a lighthouse for corporate values and build some of the networks – both internal and external – that will support innovation going forward.' Noting the greater interest being shown by new recruits, particularly graduates, in the sustainability attitudes of their employers, he sees this developing into a stronger engagement in environmental impact reduction with business partners.

For many organisations their largest impacts come in their supply chain. This is especially true for retailers and the leaders are now working closely to address environmental and social issues that arise through their supply chain. This can be complex and challenging. Julian Walker-Palin is the Head of Corporate Sustainability at the supermarket chain

Asda-Walmart. He has worked with Asda's product heads to establish an online platform called the Sustain & Save Exchange that helps their suppliers find environmental efficiencies in their own business. The scale of Asda's supply chain is enormous so the cumulative benefits could be huge. Similarly the automotive sector has significant supply chain impacts as well as those arising from use of the product itself. Jaguar Land Rover publicly launched their Environmental Innovation Strategy in 2009 explicitly considering both their operational impacts and the wider product lifecycle issues from sourcing through to end-of-life. This type of approach could in the future provide a sound base for driving new innovations around products or processes.

'Lobby whilst you innovate'

A feature of sustainability leaders is that they advocate progressive legislation and policy. This has been the case with climate change where some large corporations have lobbied for ambitious policy from government to provide confidence for future investment in carbon reduction that will enable the transition to the low carbon economy. This has often been in collaboration with other businesses through new types of organisation such as the non-governmental organisation (NGO), the Climate Group (which itself can be considered an innovative social enterprise).

Lobbying policy-makers is not only the preserve of large organisations. Toby Peters, Chief Executive of a start-up called Dearman Engines, who have developed waste heat recovery technology, says it vital to 'lobby whilst you innovate'. This is a view shared by entrepreneur Julia Groves, who is Managing Director at the Trillion Fund, which is developing a new businesses based on crowdfunding renewable energy projects.

Political sentiment for issues such as climate change may have wavered over recent years. Predictable policy and legislation is nonetheless vital to build confidence in order that both corporations and clean tech entrepreneurs can make investment in low carbon technology. In the future we anticipate more effort will be devoted to engaging policymakers on this agenda.

New collaborations and partnerships for sustainable innovation

Another trait of leading sustainability organisations is the fact they develop partnerships with NGOs, sometimes with the very activists that they historically considered adversaries. This is also leading to the creation of new types of NGOs and social enterprises. The case study on Behaviour Change illustrates that multiple stakeholders are now collaborating on innovative campaigns to influence consumers.

Collaboration and social entrepreneurs

Behaviour Change is a small social enterprise that aims to promote socially and environmentally responsible living.

David Hall established Behaviour Change, after he left the Climate Group, where he had been working on consumer engagement. Prior to this, David worked in advertising, where he won awards for transforming the perception of Skoda cars. He is therefore incredibly well placed to see that the approach and skills required to sell products to consumers are very different to those to encourage consumers to change their habits.

Collaboration is absolutely central to the Behaviour Change approach. They work with multiple stakeholders – government, local authorities, businesses and charities – on programmes to make it easier for people to lead sustainable lives. Their aim is to change behaviours and not just attitudes. Consequently, they have moved away from the large-scale campaigns with a generic message, which can appear moralising, to more focused interventions based on how consumers live. For example, Dabble with your Dinner, is a campaign that aims to help British families eat more vegetables by making simple tweaks to their existing meals. They arrived at this approach after research showed that 90% of mums cook from a repertoire of nine meals. This trend to focusing on the real behaviour of consumers, so-called ethnographic research, is only really beginning as far as sustainability is concerned but is likely to grow in the future.

www.behaviourchange.org.uk

Harnessing the innovation of your employees

Green ideas schemes are widely used across organisations. Encouraging individuals or teams to submit ideas for sustainability improvements can help employee engagement but often fail to come up with genuinely innovative or useful ideas. Designing a scheme to promote useful innovation is more difficult. This may require clear explanation of the type of innovation being sought, making resources available for both those submitting and those reviewing applications, providing feedback on all ideas and motivating rewards.

BT Group has long been recognised as a leader in both sustainability and innovation, so it's unsurprising to find that their employee ideas schemes bring these two concepts together. Openreach is the BT business that installs and maintains fibre and wire broadband services, employing around 33,000 people who install, support and maintain the connections linking tens of millions of homes and businesses. The New Ideas scheme was re-launched in October 2005 and has delivered millions of pounds in new revenue, material savings and cost avoidance. Employees submitting new ideas can win up to £30,000. The annual Challenge Cup is a team competition that encourages working across BT functions, trying to find better ways to approach any given issue. In 2012 the team that placed second out of 460 entries in the competition proposed an environmental solution called Polybase. This project has the potential to reduce the carbon impact of roadside cabinets by more than 50%. The new cabinet design, currently being trialled, uses a 60% recyclable polymer and crushed stone mix in place of concrete to create a solid base for the cabinets.

Convergence of innovation and sustainability roles

All those Sustainability Executives we spoke to agreed that innovation was a more significant part of their role and they expected this trend to continue. Nike has also explicitly linked sustainability and innovation with impressive results – they have been recognised as the world's most innovative company in 2013.[30]

Fund for sustainable innovation

Dedicating specific funds for innovation activity is widely adopted as good practice. This approach has also been used at M&S for sustainability projects that may not meet current financial paybacks but have big sustainability benefits. In 2013, Patagonia, the outdoor clothing company that has been at the forefront of sustainability for many years, went further than a simple innovation fund when it set aside $20 million in its own venture capital company. Patagonia will look to invest in companies with strong environmental credentials in areas of clothing, food, water, energy and waste.

2. New products and services

A great example of new product innovation is provided by the case study on P&G's Ariel Excel Gel washing liquid, which was developed using open innovation and resulted in a dramatically improved environmental performance and superior cleaning.

Procter and Gamble (P&G) – New product innovation

P&G were one of the first organisations to embrace open innovation (see their dedicated site **www.pgconnectdevelop.com**).[31] This focus on innovation is reflected in their ambitious sustainability strategy. In 2007 they set a goal to develop $50 billion in Sustainable Innovation Products (SIPs), which are products that have a significantly reduced (>10%) environmental footprint compared to a previous or alternative version of the product. In 2012 the cumulative sales of SIPs was over $52 billion.[32]

Dr Peter White, Director of Global Sustainability, says 'innovation is the lifeblood' of P&G. As P&G has moved to think about how to

---

turn sustainability into an opportunity so innovation has become a more significant part of his role. P&G has explicitly made innovation part of the role of the Advisory Panels that form a part of their stakeholder engagement plans and they have also included an assessment of the contribution to innovation into their assessment of suppliers.

A great example of how P&G used sustainability to innovate is Ariel Excel Gel,[33] a washing machine detergent. P&G knew from Life Cycle Assessments that up to 85% of the energy consumed in the detergent's life cycle was the result of the use of hot water by the consumer during the washing phase. The challenge was to create a new product that significantly improved energy (and greenhouse gas emissions) per wash without compromising the cleaning performance.

Collaboration was evident at every stage of the process. P&G worked with its suppliers to create a new concentrated detergent (reduces waste and impacts from transportation) that used fewer source ingredients and was effective at low temperatures (i.e. 30°C or less). P&G also had to work with washing machine manufacturers to ensure that low temperature functions would be widely available on the appliances. Finally, when they launched a new product they created campaigns in partnership with not-for-profit organisations to provide awareness of the benefits to consumers.

The new detergent has proved to be a commercial success for P&G, as Peter summarises, 'Ariel Excel Gel is a classic no "trade-offs" where the consumer gets a better product and good value, and where you can see many benefits for the environment.'

The biggest challenge, having created a great product, is to get the consumers to use it at the correct temperature. P&G estimate that up to 40% of global machine loads are being washed in cold water today, there is still some way to go to achieve the goal of 70% by 2020.[32]

Interserve, a FTSE 250 construction company, has recently published an ambitious sustainability strategy. One of the goals is to support the creation of a culture of innovation. Richard Jones, Associate Director for Sustainable Business, explains how they are going to do this: 'We know reducing our carbon footprint by 50% is very, very ambitious and we will need a lot of new thinking to achieve this. Our first step is to set managers targets for their own business carbon footprints. We want them to devise ways of achieving this for themselves before the challenge is rolled out across their business.'

They already have a great example of innovative thinking that involves taking an idea from one domain and transplanting it to another. When faced with a 25% cut in the agreed budget for building the Leeds East Academy, Interserve needed to develop a new approach. Starting from a cost and resource efficiency perspective, they considered what space was needed to deliver school services and then, of course, what wasn't so important. Their answer was to focus on the classrooms and minimize the space devoted to corridors. Adopting the modular concepts seen in mobile offices (Podsolve) and applying this approach resulted in a building that is not only lower in upfront cost but also cheaper to maintain with less space to heat, light and cool.

Developing new products will require a deep understanding of target markets and in particular the role of social media in people's lives. Pete Markey, Chief Marketing Officer for RSA Insurance Group, describes a recent initiative using Facebook that allows someone to recruit a group of friends who can then obtain more favourable home insurance terms. Although it resembles bulk buying practice it actually represents a better proposition to the insurer since the members are likely to select only friends with a similar risk profile to themselves. This is a group of friends who know each other and are unlikely to issue an invite to, for example, a friend who is a careless driver since that would jeopardise their end of year bonus.

Not all innovative products or services are commercially successful. Sometimes the product's sustainability credentials may not be good enough, as was the case with first generation biofuels. In other cases, consumers may be slow to adopt the new technology, for example, electric cars, or new business models such as the electric car battery change idea developed by Better Place. GreenWheels was a green car insurance product, which one of the authors worked on, that was before its time. Based on the black box in-car technology it used a web interface to identify individual ecodriving style. It was technologically advanced and offered both green and financial benefits to customers and insurers. GreenWheels also allowed drivers to benchmark their driving style via the web. This product is no longer available but given the huge increase in social media it may well be an attractive proposition once more.

3. New business models

New businesses

There are many companies that have been set up to sell new technology or services that have environmental benefits – ranging from renewable energy to pollution abatement equipment. As noted in the introduction there has also been a rapid proliferation of social enterprises, a fascinating topic in itself but beyond the scope of this publication. Earth Capital Partners is an example of a new type of business that focuses on sustainability in the often conservative world of investment management.

Earth Capital Partners

In 2008 Stanley Fink set up an asset management company focusing on sustainable investment. Earth Capital Partners offers an investment model, which prioritises sustainable development alongside financial return, delivering commercial risk-adjusted returns to investors. In establishing a new model for asset management, it was critical to build a team that not only shared Lord Fink's ambitious vision but also had the skills necessary to manage funds in this emerging asset class.

ECP Partner James Stacey explains that by selecting appropriate segments of the sustainable investment opportunity set, attractive risk adjusted returns are available right across the risk spectrum, from early stage venture capital through to 'steady state' infrastructure. The key factor is understanding the market, notably the commercial drivers and policy direction and

---

interventions. For example, ECP's focus to date towards renewable energy infrastructure and sustainable timberland offer steady relatively predictable double-digit returns with a low correlation to conventional asset classes and good correlation to inflation – attractive features in the current market.

By ensuring that financial return is not compromised, ECP has been able to attract a breadth of investment talent, experience and capability. Knowing that the business only invests in assets which contribute positively to Sustainable Development provides an additional motivation for the team over and above what they have previously experienced.

Earth Capital Partners has been recognised and rewarded for its sustainable investment innovation and successes. This has included an Upper Quartile ranking (highest ranking possible) for sustainable investment by the United Nations Principles for Responsible Investment (UN PRI); The Mergers and Acquisitions International 'UK Sustainable Finance Adviser of the Year 2012'; and the 'UK Specialist Group of 2013' in the International Hedge Fund Awards.

There are also two trends that are starting to lead to disruptive start-ups and changes in the business models of large corporations:

- The circular economy, or closed-loop manufacturing
- Collaborative consumption

The emergence of the circular economy (TCE)

The work of the Ellen MacArthur Foundation and its partners is now pushing this concept into the mainstream. Early sustainability pioneers have arrived at the same conclusion as TCE – closed-loop manufacturing dramatically reduces environmental impacts and dependence on scarce resources. Their reports provide a compelling argument for this (see the excellent Foundation reports[34]) but it requires a dramatic change to business models. It's not only designing products that can readily be dismantled and recycled at end-of-life but also a new system for collecting the old products. Such a model naturally lends itself to businesses that sell a service rather than just a product.

For executives looking at making the case for adopting TCE principles we strongly recommend the Ellen MacArthur Foundation, with its programme of executive development to support implementation.

The closed and open ecosystem terminology used to explain the different approaches of Apple and Google to technology provides a strong analogy to the two main strategic options for TCE:

- 'closed ecosystem', where a company seeks to only recover their products through their own supply chain;

- 'open ecosystem' where a company is happy to reuse any sustainable material.

The early adopter in a sector may by necessity be forced, at least initially, to a 'closed ecosystem' approach. Whichever approach is selected will have dramatic implications for companies working in the supply chain. It will also have an impact on regional or national government policy

– an open ecosystem approach may be preferred as it may create the opportunity to create centres of excellence of new types of businesses. Executives working through a strategy for TCE will also need to think about which products or services they start with and over which geography. It may be easier for new products and services than those already on offer.

The Kyocera Corporation approach to sustainability aligns with TCE thinking. Building on its core competence of technical ceramics Kyocera has built up a portfolio of global businesses ranging from solar panels through to document management systems. Its management philosophy, dating back to its founding in 1959, is that its business should coexist harmoniously with nature and society. This philosophy underpins the sustainability initiatives within the company including the product-service shift model they have pioneered in document management services. This innovation moves the focus away from the hardware (devices) to the delivery of the documents themselves.

Tracey Rawling Church, Head of CSR, Kyocera Document Solutions (UK), explains that conventional laser print technology relies on a drum that is replaced every time the toner runs out. By developing a hard-wearing amorphous silicon drum Kyocera removed the necessity of frequent drum replacement. This makes Kyocera toner cassettes much less complex and costly than the conventional alternative, because all the moving parts are housed permanently in the printer instead of being part of the consumable. Minimising the number of print devices required coupled with training on use of energy/paper saving features, pay-per-page pricing and recycling provides quantifiable energy and paper savings as well as a reduction in overall spend. Of course, like any disruptive innovation there are always significant barriers to be overcome. The corporate tender process itself can stifle innovation if, as often happens, it is written around hardware specification rather than the desired outcome of the project. This results in a competition that focuses on hardware discounts rather than the value of the service itself. The green benefits are sometimes missed if the relevant sustainability team isn't fully aligned with the procurement function. Kyocera may offer products that are more resource efficient and more easily dismantled and reprocessed at end-of-life but this doesn't add cost, rather it supports improved value for the customer – as long as they appreciate the long-term value of the proposition.

Moving forward, Tracey sees more opportunities for this type of approach; huge benefits could be realised, for example, if silos that exist between government departments were overcome to provide a more collaborative, integrated approach to document management. She says, 'I'm certain that hardware-led procurement leads to expensive mistakes, where current equipment is just replaced with something more up to date when the most resource-efficient and cost-effective solution would be a document management service. But the product-service shift requires adaptation on the part of purchasers as well as suppliers if its benefits are to be fully realised.'

Collaborative consumption

Collaborative consumption[35] is a social movement, enabled by the Internet, that delivers economic benefits to those with goods to share and those who want to borrow them. This is a significant economic phenomenon that includes large businesses such as Ebay and many exciting start-ups – the collaborative consumption website has a directory of services that covers well-known accommodation sites (e.g. Airbnb), transport (e.g. car share and bike hire) to social dining and tool sharing.

From a sustainability perspective, the shift from 'ownership' to 'sharing' has huge benefits through reduced use of natural resources. This is not the first example of new services being made possible by the low transaction costs of the Internet. What is really interesting is what this tells us about the social nature of the web and the importance of peer-to-peer review.

'Sharing' business models depend on trust between strangers. This is achieved by allowing both the party renting and the sellers to evaluate one another. Social networks enable further due diligence to be undertaken by both parties, as well as means of spreading positive experiences. For those interested in sustainability, collaborative consumption is an important and welcome trend. It also represents a real challenge for companies as customers can link to customers. Leading brands have begun to experiment with new sharing services, for example General Motors are now trailing a car sharing service.

One of our favourite examples is M&S's Shwopping campaign (see case study). This combines TCE with collaborative consumption whilst using social media to engage consumers.

M&S Shwop

In 2012 Marks & Spencer (M&S) launched their 'Shwopping' campaign where consumers were encouraged to bring in old items of clothing when they shopped. Later in the year M&S then sold a women's coat, which had been remade from the returned

---

items. This is a really interesting example of a major brand developing a closed loop approach to manufacturing. This required considerable innovation around developing a reverse supply chain – i.e. establishing new logistic processes for the collection, sorting and dispatch of old clothing. It also needed technical innovation in their supply chain to ensure that the manufacturing process could reuse recovered fibre.

However, perhaps the most interesting thing about shwopping was the attempt to engage the consumer. This non-product campaign incorporated a highly innovative social media strategy alongside other forms of media and PR activity. Each piece of advertising carried a QR code that linked through to M&S's Facebook page where the consumer could download an app which allowed them to share their experiences and compete for badges and prizes. In addition to being an example of the circular economy, Shwopping also gives M&S a foot in the door in the sharing economy. It will be fascinating to see how this progresses in future.

Challenge of engaging the consumer

Notwithstanding any effort to develop a sustainable product or service there remains the huge challenge of achieving market acceptance and getting the consumer to use the product properly. Paul Polman, CEO of Unilever, has publicly discussed the challenge of getting consumers to purchase refills for washing liquid bottles. It is also the case that most consumers don't wash their clothes at 30°C despite buying a cleaning product that works at this temperature. Mike Barry, Head of Sustainable

Business at M&S, summarises this by saying, 'we know how to build the rocket but now we need to train the astronauts'.

Social media is transforming the relationship between brands and their customers. In his book *Who Cares Wins*, David Jones made the point that social media is also forcing businesses to be more socially responsible.[36] Environmental campaigners have a strong track record in mobilising support for one-off issues and campaigns using social media. However, to date social media hasn't been effectively used to engage mainstream consumers in changing their behaviour. Partly this is because sustainability communications follow a traditional broadcast approach that targets everyone with the same message, frequently in the form of a list of 'things-to-do', or more often 'not-to-do'. Social media encourages conversations and this is different to broadcasting or advertising.

Collaborative consumption shows that we can use new technology to shape and change social norms. Using social media and existing social networks for peer-to-peer reviews could be vital in developing markets for 'greener' products and services. Such approaches would also re-build trust amongst consumers who are deeply cynical about 'green' claims from brands. This may require the sustainability leaders, brands and social enterprises, to work collectively and also to embrace co-creation with advocates so they feel properly engaged.

Influencing consumer behaviour is more challenging than getting them to buy a product. It is time to re-think how we communicate sustainability with a mainstream audience. Part of the reason we find 'Shwopping' so appealing is that M&S are attempting to engage consumers using social media.

System change

'System change' is a phrase one hears often in the sustainability community. This recognises that transformational change requires action by many parties. Forum for the Future has set itself the challenging goal of supporting system-wide change towards a sustainable future. Anna Birney, who heads up the System Innovation Lab, explains, 'we aim to create interventions which add up to a shift in the whole system. This requires more of organisations than simply changing their internal practices – it means they need to work with others to support wider change.' Examples of current projects include Dairy 2020 which brings together the whole of the supply chain to identify potential futures for the industry, supported by guiding principles on how to achieve desired sustainability outcomes.

By definition, the scale of change required for system change is outside of the influence of any one organisation. To be successful it will require organisations to share intellectual property not just with external collaborators through open innovation, but everyone including competitors – they will need to act as platforms to enable more innovation rather than institutions that protect their own interests. New technology in itself will however be insufficient; it will require changes in consumer habits, government regulation and incentives, industrial networks and infrastructure.

CHAPTER 5

Implementing Sustainable Innovation

IN THIS CHAPTER WE CONSIDER how Sustainability Executives can take practical steps to manage innovation. Where the organisation currently lies in terms of the three phases of sustainability is a key factor in determining appropriate actions. As organisations develop more ambitious sustainability strategies then so the importance of innovation in the role of the sustainability function will increase. It is not only the imperative for innovation that changes but also the type of innovation required.

Sustainability Executives need to develop new skills as they progress through the phases and this is summarised in Table 1. Moreover, it is not only the sustainability personnel who need to develop new skills: the whole organisation must have both sustainability and innovation embedded in their roles to reach the challenging second and third phases. Executives and managers outside a central sustainability function will need to have a working understanding of the sustainability impacts of their current role along with emerging opportunities. This is a huge step to take. There are numerous courses available that provide an introduction to sustainability issues and some excellent initiatives aimed at engaging senior level executives but coaching and mentoring approaches are likely to be more effective than conventional training given time pressures and the role-specific nature of the learning required.

TABLE 1. Summary of how innovation and skills change through sustainability levels

Level 1: Compliance, cost saving & reputation	Level 2: New products and services	Level 3: Systemic
Innovation opportunity	*Innovation opportunity*	*Innovation opportunity*
Low opportunity for innovation. Focus on adopting best practice across operations generally using established technology or trials of new technology against existing business case criteria.	Using social and environmental insight to create new products and services. Working across internal departments and with external partners.	Develop new business models – ranging from 'sharing' service-based models instead of just selling a product to new businesses or social enterprises to address sustainability challenges. Challenges the way the organisation operates and its willingness to invest in collaborations with multiple parties to encourage a transition.
Skills needed	*Skills needed*	*Skills needed*
Emphasis and command and control processes – standards and total quality management. Understanding of current legislation and how to influence future legislation. Understand existing technology solutions in supply chain and quickly trial new technology. External reporting of non-financial performance. Supply chain programme focused on social and environment performance of suppliers operations. Stakeholder engagement plan. Participate in sector initiatives with rival companies.	Understand life-cycle impacts of existing products. Ability to inspire and manage a collaboration of internal and external specialists. Network of potential innovation partners that extends beyond current supply chain and sector. Consumer insight and ability to create new value or service type propositions. Predict market opportunity and develop an implementation strategy. Collaborate on cross-sectoral sustainability initiatives. Protect intellectual property.	Knowledge of setting up new businesses. Change management. Brand management. Develop a new market – how to gain consumer insight and shape their behaviour. Large network outside of organisation. Advocate progressive public policy. Build trust with third parties. Establish a platform to promote and encourage further innovation.

Note: The structure of this table follows that provided in the paper 'Why sustainability is now the key driver for innovation' in *Harvard Business Review*.[37] Although we have changed the content, we thoroughly recommend this paper.

It is not surprising that the organisations that are considered leaders in sustainability are also often at the forefront of innovation. Sustainability functions in such organisations are able to use existing innovation processes to support sustainability goals. However, we have found Sustainability Executives in these organisations are also starting to use stakeholder engagement and supply chain programmes explicitly for purposeful conversations about sustainable innovations. Another feature of the leaders is that they will have separate funds available for investing in projects or initiatives that may not meet the mainstream business case requirements – in other words, a separate sustainable innovation fund.

The majority of Sustainability Executives will be working in businesses that are in the first phases of sustainability and have a very operational focus so that innovation processes are less developed. Here the challenge will be to gain both senior executive commitment and resources. So what should executives in this position being doing?

Undertake a review. A useful initial step is to review the current processes and performance of your organisation in terms of both sustainability and innovation. Is there a clear link to overall strategic objectives? Does the company culture encourage both internal and external collaboration? Consider lessons learnt from recent successes and failures.

Don't rely on green ideas schemes. Most organisations have suggestion boxes for environmental improvements and many run small green ideas schemes. This approach has a role to play in engaging the workforce but in our experience yield little in terms of good ideas, which is why they generally are soon forgotten. Command-and-control systems, such as management standards like ISO14001, can help deliver incremental improvements but, as we explain in Chapter 3, more ambitious innovation requires a different approach. Don't abandon the ideas schemes but seek to get resources to get cross-functional teams working on bigger challenges.

Provide a focus for the innovation you are looking for. Open-ended requests for innovation don't work for most organisations – it's true Google allow staff to work on their own projects for up to 10% of their time but most organisations find that if they define the challenges they need addressing and which link to strategic roles, then they get better results.

Set ambitious targets. As we saw with Interserve in Chapter 4, if you ask for a 25% improvement then you are more likely to come up with a new approach than if you ask for 5% which encourage incremental tweaking.

Encourage collaborations across teams. It can be extremely challenging in organisations where collaboration across departments is not incentivised to get other departments to release staff to work on innovation challenges. In this situation Sustainability Executives may need to demonstrate how addressing the challenge will benefit the different departments and be prepared to let them take the credit. Having a clear focus on a challenge to be addressed and the potential benefits will help in these discussions.

Develop external networks. Purposely look to connect with new organi-sations that may be working in areas that could support your innovation aspirations. Add the topic of innovation to your stakeholder engagement activities – this can be part intelligence gathering, part foundation for external collaboration. Also, in supply chain programmes, which typically specify sustainability standards, start asking for innovative approaches that can deliver significant performance improvements. This could be in forums or in tender documents.

Look outside of sustainability. It is important to track best practice in sustainability but actively look outside the discipline for new trends and opportunities. The circular economy work run by the Ellen MacArthur Foundation is finding great success by engaging a new audience. Collaborative consumption is a social trend that although it has enormous sustainability benefits was not created by the sustainability profession. In the last chapter we provide some interesting trends to watch for in sustainable innovation.

Establish yourself as an innovative thinker. The role of the Sustainability Executive should be about creating the correct framework to promote, encourage and nurture innovation rather than personal creativity. However, in the early phases when the Sustainability Executive is seeking to gain support for more ambitious strategies, then gaining confidence of the executive team is important. A really effective way to do this is to start reporting on trends – consumer insight, new technology, developments in competitors or non-sector leaders – in your monthly reports. Also, send through relevant information to executives and heads of department and follow up to see if there is any opportunity or appetite for change. Several years ago, one of the authors, who certainly was not a digital native at the time, reported on a trend around use of smart phones to access local information in his report to the senior executive team. This unexpectedly resulted in him leading a project to look at the implications for the business. This approach will also hopefully help identify allies for change internally and people who you can work with on new initiatives.

Make the most of internal changes. Both authors have found that the arrival of a new Chief Executive can be a great opportunity to gain more commitment and support for their agenda. Generally, a new Chief

Executive is keen to do things differently from their predecessor, so do your homework about how they operate – for example, do they like the big vision or quantified data? They will, in our experience, want to change vision and values to create a new culture. Sustainability Executives are well placed to lead on this work or at least provide significant input, so make sure you get involved. It may be necessary to rethink how you position sustainability to support the new agenda and ambitions – be prepared to do things slightly differently. On a cautionary note, we have also both experienced how it is not necessarily the case that a new Chief Executive will show greater commitment to sustainability and it can be the reverse.

There are other opportunities that can be exploited to drive the agenda forward. Rebranding is great chance to talk about the big picture issues and leading brands are increasingly defining a clear 'sense of purpose'; new market research is a good chance to try and get more detailed information on consumer behaviour and attractiveness of new sustainable products or innovation; similarly, the acquisition or creation of new business can be a good time for new thinking.

There are many similarities in the management approaches to innovation and sustainability and both face similar challenges achieving integration into core management processes. The Sustainability Executive is well placed to support or even lead on mainstream innovation. The social and environmental agenda is about the 'big picture' and provides the 'meaning of life' type questions that are important in creating a sense of purpose. The Sustainability Executive will typically be very comfortable in working with concerns around transparency, many will have argued successfully for greater voluntary disclosure of performance data. They will also have networks that extend to organisations outside the company and may even be working collaboratively with them on different projects.

Innovation and sustainability are becoming more closely aligned and both are essential for business survival and future prosperity. Understanding sustainability should provide opportunities to stimulate new opportunities while also being a filter that should help companies select the innovation with the greatest chance of success.

....

CHAPTER 6

Concluding Thoughts

THE WORLD IS VERY DIFFERENT from when Peter Drucker wrote his seminal book predicting the entrepreneurial society in the 1980s:[11] globalisation has led to fierce competition and made the world smaller and organisations are flatter and increasingly collaborate externally. The pace of technological progress is accelerating and resulting in greater uncertainty. Climate change and growing concern over limited natural resources have emerged and led to the discipline of sustainability.

We hope to have provided a framework in order to understand the role innovation has in sustainability. The sustainability literature too often focuses on how companies do things (i.e. visions, processes, reporting) rather than what they do (i.e. their products or services). The emphasis of sustainability should be about 'what you do' not 'how you do it'. Russell Ackoff noted: 'Peter Drucker made a great distinction between doing things right and doing the right thing. All our societal problems arise out of doing the wrong thing righter. The more efficient you are at doing the wrong thing the wronger you become. It is much better to do the right thing wronger than the wrong thing righter! If you do the right thing wrong and correct it you get better.'[38] In time the assessment of corporate sustainability will focus on 'what you do' and metrics for quantifying sustainable innovations will be developed.

Many major innovations that have led to sustainability benefits did not originally arise from some sustainability motivation. The sharing economy is a good example. But the examples of P&G and M&S in Chapter 4 show that leading companies are now using sustainability insight as source of innovation. Sustainability will also increasingly be used as a filter by organisations as they seek to select the innovation with the greatest chance of success. Innovation and sustainability are becoming more closely aligned and both are essential for business survival and future prosperity.

Niels Bohr said, 'prediction, especially about the future, is very difficult'. Predictions about the future can also date very quickly, or as *The Economist* more eloquently puts it, 'nothing ages faster than yesterday's dreams of tomorrow'.[39] Nonetheless, a strong working knowledge of new technology and social trends will enable the Sustainability Executive to be better placed to engage and influence strategic discussion. Before we list some emerging innovations our final caveat is that impact of a new innovation such as the cloud or digital technology will vary according to the sector.

Some interesting technologies that have huge potential to be both disruptive and sustainable include:

- Big data
- The 'internet of things'
- Crowdsourcing
- Biomimicry
- Mobile social networks

- Developments in biological and material sciences

- Renewable energy

- Electric cars, fuel cells or both?

- 3-D printing, localised manufacturing and the maker movement

However, equally important will be the need to engage and influence the behaviour of consumers. Even our most favoured brands find it difficult to change our habits but 'training the astronauts' is vital if we are to create a demand for more sustainable goods and services. Social media has empowered consumers and combined with 'big data' allows us to gain a much deeper understanding of consumer behaviour. The trick will be to know the right questions to ask and things to measure. We will see a shift from questionnaires that track attitudes to ethnographic data (Behaviour Change case study). This will allow us to treat consumers as individuals with different motivations and challenges before we seek to 'nudge' them towards more desirable behaviour. Empowered social media-savvy consumers are showing an appetite for co-creating new products with brands while the sharing economy is linking consumers to each other.

Innovation is inherently risky. Not all 'good' ideas actually result in 'good' products or services. As the sustainable innovation agenda moves forward we must therefore expect to see more failures, and strange as this sounds failures, such as the electric car business Better Place, will be a sign that sustainability is succeeding. Sustainability leaders will embrace modern innovation theory about lean start-up, rapid prototyping and even co-creation of products with consumers. There is great interest in systemic change. No single organisation will be able to manage such transitions. Technology transitions involve many parties and high degree of interconnectivity. The degree to which transitions are emergent properties or can be directed will remain to be seen. What is clear is that this must involve a range of organisations from government, academia, private sector (some fierce competitors) and civil society. Private corporations are getting used to open innovation but will now have to look for an even more radical change and openness around intellectual property if they are truly committed to system innovation – it will require them to operate as enabling platforms for further innovation, not institutions that protect their own interests.

Peter Drucker considered management to be a technology as it was capable of profound changes in attitudes, values and behaviour. This is a worthy ambition for sustainability. Sustainability is ultimately concerned with transforming how organisations and economies operate, which is why we are beginning to see a convergence of sustainability and innovation.
....

References

Introduction

1. Breakthrough Capitalism: http://www.breakthroughcapitalism.com

2. Elkington, J. 2012. *The Zeronauts: Breaking the Sustainability Barrier* (Abingdon: Routledge).

3. Stanford Social Innovation: www.ssireview.org

4. Elkington, J. & Hartigan, P. 2008. *The Power of Unreasonable People: How Social Entrepreneurs Create Markets that Change the World* (Cambridge, MA: Harvard Business School Press).

Chapter 1

5. Anderson, R. with White, R. 2009. *Confessions of a Radical Industrialist* (New York: Random House Business Books).

6. Elkington, J. 2012. *The Zeronauts: Breaking the Sustainability Barrier* (Abingdon: Routledge).

7. BT, 2013. *Better Future Report*: www.btplc.com/betterfuture/betterbusiness/betterfuturereport/report/NG.aspx

8. Porter, M.E. & Kramer, M.R. 2011. Creating shared value. *Harvard Business Review*, January–February.

9. Detailed information on the circular economy is available at the Ellen MacArthur Foundation: www.ellenmacarthurfoundation.org. Highly recommended are the two reports they have published on 'Towards the circular economy'.

10. http://www.fastcompany.com/most-innovative-companies/2013/nike

Chapter 2

11. Drucker, P. 2007. *Innovation and Entrepreneurship* (Classic Drucker Collection) (Oxford: Butterworth-Heinemann).

12. Disruptive Innovation – the MOOC (2013), blog at **www.sand-walk.org**

13. Christensen, C. 1997. *The Innovator's Dilemma: When New Technology Causes Great Firms to Fail* (Cambridge, MA: Harvard Business School Press).

14. Downes, L. and Nunes, P.F. 2013. Big-bang disruption. *Harvard Business Review*, March.

15. Radjou, N., Prabhu, J. and Ahuja, S. 2012. *Jugaad Innovation: Think Frugal, Be Flexible, Generate Breakthrough Growth* (San Francisco, CA: Jossey Bass).

16. Jaideep Prabhu University of Cambridge iUniversity course.

17. Chesborough, H. 2003. *Open Innovation: The New Imperative for Creating and Profiting from Technology* (Cambridge, MA: Harvard Business School Press).

18. Chesborough, H. 2011. *Open Service Innovation: Rethinking Your Business to Grow and Compete in a New Era* (San Francisco, CA: Jossey Bass).

19. **www.openinnovation.net**

20. Ries, E. 2008. *The Lean Startup: How Today's Entrepreneurs Use Continuous Innovation to Create Radically Successful Businesses* (New York: Crown Business Publishing).

21. Lafley, G. and Charan, R. 2008. *The Game-Changer: How You Can Drive Revenue and Profit Growth with Innovation* (New York: Crown Business Publishing).

22. Kelley, T. and Littman, J. 2002. *The Art of Innovation: Success through Innovation the IDEO Way* (London: Profile Books).

23. Miller, P. and Wedell-Wedellsborg, T. 2013. *Innovation as Usual: How to Help*

Your People Bring Great Ideas to Life (Cambridge, MA: Harvard Business School Publishing).

24. Johnson, S. 2010. *Where Good Ideas Come From. The Seven Patterns of Innovation* (London: Penguin Books).

Chapter 3

25. Miller, P. and Wedell-Wedellsborg, T. 2013. *Innovation as Usual: How to Help Your People Bring Great Ideas to Life* (Cambridge, MA: Harvard Business School Publishing).

26. Gratton, L. 2007. *Hot Spots – Why Some Companies Buzz with Energy and Innovation and Others Don't* (London: FT/Prentice Hall).

27. Bain & Company. 2012. Survey on Corporate Sustainability and Philanthropy 2012. **http://www.bain.com/about/press/press-releases/employee-sustainability-study-press-release.aspx**

28. EDF and Business in the Community. 2010. *Leadership Skills for a Sustainable Economy.* **http://www.ipsos-mori.com/researchpublications/researcharchive/2634/Leadership-Skills-for-a-Sustainable-Economy.aspx**

29. European Commission. 2011. Ecoinnovation/resource efficiency survey: **http://ec.europa.eu/environment/working_en.htm**

Chapter 4

30. **http://www.fastcompany.com/most-innovative-companies/2013/nike**

31. Lafley, A.G. and Charan, R. 2008. *The Game-Changer: How You Can Drive Revenue and Profit Growth with Innovation* (New York: Crown Business Publishing).

32. P&G 2012 Sustainability Report **http://www.pg.com/en_US/downloads/sustainability/reports/PG_2012_Sustainability_Overview.pdf.**

33. World Business Council for Sustainable Development. 2012. Collaboration,

innovation, transformation Ideas and inspiration to accelerate sustainable growth – A value chain approach **http://www.wbcsd.org/Pages/EDocument/ EDocumentDetails.aspx?ID=14257&NoSearchContextKey=true**

34. Detailed information on the circular economy is available at the Ellen MacArthur Foundation: **www.ellenmacarthurfoundation.org**. Highly recommended are the two reports they have published on 'Towards the circular economy'.

35. Botsman, R. and Roger, R. 2011. *What's Mine is Yours: How Collaborative Consumption is Changing the Way We Live* (London: Collins).

36. Jones, D. 2012. *Who Cares Wins: Why Good Business is Better Business* (London: FT Publishing).

Chapter 5

37. Nidumolu, R., Prahalad, C.K. and Rangaswami, M.R. 2009. Why sustainability is now the key driver of innovation. *Harvard Business Review*, September.

Chapter 6

38. Ackoff, R.L., Addison, H.J. and Bibb, S. 2007. *Management F-laws: How Organizations Really Work* (Axminster, Devon: Triarchy Press).

39. *The Economist.* 2013. The future technology of the past, 22 June.

....

For Product Safety Concerns and Information please contact our EU
representative GPSR@taylorandfrancis.com
Taylor & Francis Verlag GmbH, Kaufingerstraße 24, 80331 München, Germany

www.ingramcontent.com/pod-product-compliance
Ingram Content Group UK Ltd.
Pitfield, Milton Keynes, MK11 3LW, UK
UKHW040927180425
457613UK00011B/284